The Definition of Your Situation

[Part 1]

—Revised Edition—

Published

By

Edson Mazira

ISBN 978-1-77906-384-7

The Definition of Your Situation

[Part 1]

—Revised Edition—

DEDICATION

With all my heart, I completely dedicate this book to anyone in any unpleasant situation. May the grace of our God, the God of Abraham, Isaac and Jacob, come to them in abundance. Amen.

ACKNOWLEDGEMENTS

With much respect and honour, I acknowledge all my friends and relatives who support my work in different ways. May the Lord God bless them.

CONTENTS

OPENING PRAYER

Precious God, who dwells in Heaven between the cherubim, great and awesome is your name Jehovah, the Almighty Warrior, the Lion of the Tribe of Judah.

Father, the Almighty Warrior, I pray that you fight for me and deliver me from this tough situation as I peruse this book.

I pray for knowledge and deliverance from your teachings.

O my God, open my mind that I understand your Word, and guide me that I won't go astray.

In the name of Jesus Christ, I shout, "Amen!"

INTRODUCTION

LIFE is a journey with fortunes and misfortunes. When the misfortunes come in our way, we usually question if God really exists. We do so because we really believe that these are caused by spiritual beings in spiritual realms, and this is true.

This book has it all; it exposes these spiritual beings and gives insight on how to deal with them. This is the right time God is going to help you. He has not failed you. He has His ways, which are not similar to our ways [Isaiah 55 vs. 8].

You have to know that everything happens for a purpose. One day, you will sit down and tell people your story. It will surely motivate them.

May God bless you. Amen.

THE ENEMY ON EARTH

Satan is the enemy on earth that usually creates tough situations for us. Before he fell down, he was an archangel that served with his department under God the Father. His department was comprised of a third angels and a few ministering spirits serving under him.

By that time, Michael was (and is still) an archangel who served (and is still serving) under God the Son. Under Michael, there was (and there is still) a third angels and a number of ministering spirits.

Gabriel was (and is still) one of the archangels. He served (and is still serving) under God the Spirit. Under him, there was (and there is still) a third angels and a number of ministering spirits serving in his department.

Lucifer, who is now Satan, was in the Department of Praise and Worship, Michael was (and is still) in the Department of Heaven's Army [Revelation 12 vs. 7: And there was war in heaven. Michael and his angels fought against the dragon...], and Gabriel was (and is still) in the Department of Message Delivery [Luke 1 vs. 19: And the angel answering said unto him, I am Gabriel, that stand in the presence of God; and am sent to speak unto thee...

[Luke 1 vs. 26: In the sixth month, God sent the angel Gabriel to Nazareth, a town in Galilee...]

When Lucifer rebelled against God the Father, he was driven away, and he fell down onto this earth. One third of the angels and the number of the ministering spirits, which served in his department, followed him. Because God loves His creatures on earth, He warned them—Revelation 12 vs. 12: "...woe to the earth and the sea, because the devil has gone down to you! He is filled with fury, because he knows that his time is short."

An interesting piece of news is that this enemy is on earth for a short time. It shall come to pass when he will no longer torment us.

Satan and his kingdom came to live on land and in the oceans. Today, there are many of them almost everywhere. A certain man in Africa whose name I cannot disclose confessed that he once joined Satanism when he was in a tough life situation. He narrated that he was initiated into it by a friend who had offered to help him get out of the situation. That was the friend he had known for years. During his Satanism test, the man said he met the Queen of the Coast. That's the Mother of the marine spirits you always hear about; they reside in the oceans. This reminds me of a well-known story in which Jesus Christ cast out legion spirits from a mentally deranged man, who is now popularly known as 'Legion'. The desperate spirits requested to enter about 2,000 pigs, as if they needed permanent residence in them, yet they were in need of immediate transport to take them to the nearest sea where they belonged: Mark 5 vs. 12-13: 12 The demons begged Jesus, "Send us among the pigs; allow us to go into them." 13 He gave them permission, and the evil spirits came out and went into the pigs. The herd, about two thousand in number, rushed down the steep bank into the lake and were drowned.

The African man also said he was taken underground where he was tested by other spirits. Those were the spirits that operate on land. I remember a certain, sad incident that occurred to my uncle's son. One day he was pursuing a rooster, and the rooster sprinted through a clump of thorny bushes. When the boy tried to pass through those bushes, these evil spirits tackled him into epilepsy. It's bad.

These evil spirits cannot carry out their mission without using people or animals; that's why the devil used a serpent in the Garden of Eden to mislead Eve [Genesis, chapter 3]. To get rid of them, we have to receive Jesus Christ into our lives. Jesus Christ should reign in us.

Praise God! The African man I am talking about repented and received Jesus Christ as his personal saviour. He exposed all possible ways the devil uses in his Satanism Ministry. This devil is cunning. He introduces some systems on earth to trick people into worshipping him. May God have mercy on us. This enemy is evil. He inflicts people with sicknesses and diseases. He causes great confusion. He is the thief that Jesus Christ said he came to steal and kill—John 10 vs. 10: "The thief comes only to steal and kill and destroy..."

You need to get mad at him because he stole your joy and drove you into this misfortune. However, God is going to change it into a blessing. Amen.

Let us rip off this enemy's face and embarrass him.

RIPPING OFF THE FACE OF THE ENEMY

Because the devil once sought to be worshipped when he was in the Kingdom of God, he created his 'churches' on earth so that he could mislead people into his kingdom. God warned us about these 'churches'—1 Timothy 4 vs. 1-4: **1** The Spirit clearly says that in later times some will abandon the faith and follow deceiving spirits and things taught by demons. **2** Such teachings come through hypocritical liars, whose consciences have been seared as with a hot iron. **3** They forbid people to marry and order them to abstain from certain foods, which God created to be received with thanksgiving by those who believe and those who know the truth. **4** For everything God created is good, and nothing is to be rejected if it is received with thanksgiving, because it is consecrated by the word of God and prayer.

Dear friends, when the devil wants to mislead people to worship him, he can also use the Bible for reference. He once tempted Jesus Christ, using some scriptures—Matthew 4 vs. 6: "...throw yourself down. For it is written: 'He will command his angels concerning you, and they will lift you up in their hands...'"

The devil knows very well that there are areas in the Bible where God commanded people to abstain from certain foods. Hence, he refers readers to those areas, knowing he can mislead them. Right now, many people call the Bible a self-contradictory book. It is because they fail to understand it when God commanded people in the Old Testament to abstain from certain foods [Leviticus 11 vs. 1-47: **3** You may eat any animal that has a split hoof... **4** There are some that only chew the cud or only have a split hoof, but you must not eat them...], but in the New Testament, the same God warns people about misleading teachings from demons that will command people to abstain from certain foods—particularly the foods that He Himself forbad (forbid) people to eat in the Old Testament [1 Timothy 4 vs. 3-4: **3** They...order them to abstain from certain foods, which God created to be received with thanksgiving by those who believe and those who know the truth. **4** For everything God created is good, and nothing is to be rejected if it is received with thanksgiving, because it is consecrated by the word of God and prayer]. This really looks as if it's contradictory, but it's not like that at all.

The Bible is straightforward. Before Christ came, people lived under the Law of Moses, and they could be justified by God through observing it. The law had a curse attached to it, so if anyone broke it, they were cursed automatically [Galatians 3 vs. 10: All who rely on observing the law are under a curse, for it is written: "Cursed is everyone who does not continue to do everything written in the Book of the Law."] So many people lived with curses, because they couldn't observe all the laws, and that pleased the devil. Even now, the devil still wants people to worship God under the Law of Moses, because he knows they cannot manage to keep it in whole; as a result, they become cursed automatically. Sometimes our lives don't go well in churches because of this type of curse. We try to do what we cannot do. No man can be justified by observing this law [Galatians 3 vs. 11: Clearly no-one is justified before God by the law...]

Whenever the Israelites in the Bible broke any of those Laws, animals were killed for their blood to cleanse them, the Israelites. That was done repeatedly because people sinned repeatedly.

Later on, grace came by Jesus Christ. He redeemed us from the curse of the law: Galatians 3 vs. 13-14: 13 Christ redeemed us from the curse of the law by becoming a curse for us, for it is written: "Cursed is everyone who is hung on a tree." 14 He redeemed us in order that the blessing given to Abraham might come to the Gentiles through Christ Jesus, so that by faith we might receive the promise of the Spirit. Before Christ redeemed us, everyone cursed was hung on a tree to show they were cursed.

The devil rejoices when he sees that we are trying to be justified by God through observing the Law of Moses. He knows—by doing so—we are distancing ourselves from Jesus Christ, while we think we are going close to Him [Galatians 5 vs. 4: You who are trying to be justified by law have been alienated from Christ; you have fallen away from grace]. This is the case, dear friends. We can talk of the grace we no longer have—that we rejected unknowingly.

Satan misleads people in many ways. His angels are in space; they roam around and communicate with some people on earth. To some, they disguise that they are the angels from God. They look almost the same with those that were left in the Kingdom of God. God did *not* give Satan and his fallen angels horns and ugly faces because they rebelled against Him. *No.* They still look almost the same because they were created by one God. So we need to be very careful. Don't just entertain every angel. We need the Spirit of God to help us discern and distinguish these spirits.

One day, Evangelist Roncemore Mhlanga and I preached to a certain man in Bindura. The man told us that he was a prophet and had times he communicated with an angel face to face in space. He told us that his spirit usually ascended to meet the angel up there and that the angel always gave him some instructions. We didn't argue with that man, but we told him the truth about the fallen angels. The fallen angels are the angels that rebelled against God; these angels seek to be worshipped by people on earth. They are the ones some prophets communicate with without knowing they are not from God. These prophets will be shocked on the Last Day of Judgment when God, whom they think they are serving, rejects them: Matthew 7 vs. 21-23: [21] "Not everyone who says to me, 'Lord, Lord,' will enter the kingdom of heaven, but only he who does the will of my Father who is in heaven. [22] Many will say to me on that day, 'Lord, Lord, did we not prophesy in your name, and in your name drive out demons and perform many miracles?' [23] Then I will tell them plainly, 'I never knew you. Away from me, you evildoers!'"

This is very pathetic, and it shows these prophets believe right now that they are serving the true God, yet they don't know they are the deceiving spirits, not the Lord [Jeremiah 5 vs. 31: The prophets prophesy lies, the priests rule by their own authority, and my people love it this way. But what will you do in the end?].

How do you know they are the fallen angels and the evil ministering spirits? You need to read the Word of God and pray for a spirit of discernment. These evil spirits try by all means to go against God's salvation, which Jesus Christ brought for us. They mostly direct people to cling to the righteousness of law, knowing it brings curse to those that fail to follow all the laws (of Moses). The righteousness of law is parallel to the righteousness of faith, which Jesus Christ introduced to us.

These deceiving spirits instruct people to use animals' or people's blood for rituals. They don't want people to know anything about the blood of Jesus Christ, which cleanses sins that are red like crimson and makes them white like snow [Isaiah 1 vs. 18].

There is no condemnation in Jesus Christ, and those who receive Him are justified by faith, not by observing the laws (of Moses): Romans 8 vs. 1: Therefore, there is now no condemnation for those who are in Christ Jesus...

The fallen angels sometimes instruct their prophets to use ocean water for certain prayers; they know there are marine spirits in the oceans. So they initiate people through that way. If you take the ocean water for general use, it has no spiritual effect at all, but if you take it for religious use, the marine spirits accompany you.

Watch out for the teachings that oppose the righteousness of faith, which Jesus Christ gave us. Discern every spirit [1 John 4 vs. 1-3: 1 Dear friends, do not believe every spirit, but test the spirits to see whether they are from God, because many false prophets have gone into the world. 2 This is how you can recognise the Spirit of God: Every spirit that acknowledges that Jesus Christ has come in the flesh is from God, 3 but every spirit that does not acknowledge Jesus is not from God. This is the spirit of the antichrist, which you have heard is coming and even now is already in the world].

Sometimes, when we know the true Gospel of Jesus Christ, we find it hard to leave those 'churches' our parents or husbands introduced to us. This situation is tough; it leaves us indecisive. We fear to lose our families and everything. But this fear profits us nothing [Mark 8 vs. 36: What good is it for a man to gain the whole world, yet forfeit his soul?]. If you are in this vexing situation, just pray to God so that He can guide you in every step. Don't fear anything. You are not alone. God chose you to save your family. The Son of Man came to save the lost [Matthew 18 vs. 11: The Son of Man came to save what was lost].

A person needs to be born again: John 3 vs. 3-7: 3 "...I tell you the truth, no-one can see the kingdom of God unless he is born again." 5 "...I tell you the truth, no-one can enter the kingdom of God unless he is born of water and the Spirit. 6 Flesh gives birth to flesh, but the Spirit gives birth to spirit. 7 You should not be surprised at my saying, 'You must be born again.'"

If a god you worship does not give you time to be born again, or if the way they say you are born again is different from the one Jesus Christ said, put a question mark.

SITUATIONS CAUSED OR ALLOWED BY GOD

Sometimes, God creates tough situations for us, but He does so to make us great, whereas the devil does it to hinder our success.

Let me tell you about some people in the Bible for whom God created challenging situations. Maybe their stories will answer yours today.

1 Samuel, chapter 9 [Samuel Anoints Saul]

God created a problem in Kish's household, and the problem affected Saul, Kish's son. God wanted to anoint Saul to be a king, but Saul couldn't move away from a comfort zone of his father's wealth. Hence, God caused Kish's donkeys to get lost, and Kish—though he had many servants to send—sent his son to search for them; he asked one of the servants to accompany him (Saul). That was vice versa. There are certain times in life when God gives us loads (or situations) that we all think should be shouldered by pagans. When this happens, we all complain and say God is not fair, but this is not so. Everything that happens happens for a certain purpose. Amen.

On the first day, Saul left home for his assignment. One of the servants accompanied him, but he, the servant, was not the owner of the assignment. With his servant, he searched through the hill country of Ephraim and through all the areas around Shalisha, but the donkeys were nowhere to be found. They went on into the District of Shaalim, but the animals were not there. Then he passed through the territory of Benjamin, but they did not find them.

5 When they reached the District of Zuph, Saul said to the servant, "Come, let's go back, or my father will stop thinking about the donkeys and start worrying about us."

Saul said that after he had tried his best and had run around for nothing. Like many of us, the young man hoped if he missed it at A, he would get it at B. Dear friends, life does not always give results as we are all pleased, but as God is. We all hope if we miss it this year, we will get it next year. But alas, the next year comes and passes by without us having achieved our goals. This is very painful, and some of us end up giving up.

It is very important in life to share our situations. Don't despise people because you don't know whom God uses for your breakthrough. Many times God uses the despised. In the case of Saul, He used Saul's servant. When Saul thought of going back, his servant suggested they visit a man of God who lived in that town:

5 ...Saul said to the servant who was with him, "Come, let's go back, or my father will stop thinking about the donkeys and start worrying about us."

6 But the servant replied, "Look, in this town there is a man of God; he is highly respected, and everything he says comes true. Let's go there now. Perhaps he will tell us what way to take."

Saul did not despise his servant. He could have turned down his suggestion, but he did not do so. Sometimes we miss our blessings because we select the people to respect. Someone you despise has got something for you. Repent.

When they reached the place of the man of God, they were told not to worry about the donkeys [1 Samuel 9 vs. 20: As for the donkeys you lost three days ago, do not worry about them; they have been found]. Samuel, the man of God, also told them that they would meet two men who would tell them that the donkeys they were looking for had been found: 1 Samuel 10 vs. 2: When you leave me today, you will meet two men near Rachel's tomb, at Zelzah on the border of Benjamin. They will say to you, 'The donkeys you set out to look for have been found. And now your father has stopped thinking about them and is worried about you. He is asking, "What shall I do about my son?"'

That was God's plan for Saul to consider His priority first. If Saul had chosen to ignore God, he would have spent years looking for the donkeys without finding them.

It is very important for us to know what God wants us to do first before we can get what we are looking for. We miss our blessings simply because we overlook certain things. God wants us to seek first His kingdom and His righteousness [Matthew 6 vs. 33: But seek first his kingdom and his righteousness, and all these things will be given to you as well].

Another occasion is of Jonah. Jonah decided not to go where God had instructed him to go.

Jonah, chapter 1 [Jonah flees from the Lord]

God sent Jonah to preach in Nineveh where people had become too wicked. But Jonah ran away from God and headed for Tarshish. He went down to Joppa where he found a ship for his journey. After paying for it, he went aboard and sailed for Tarshish. Because of that, God sent a great storm. The storm rose so violently that it threatened to break up the ship. Every sailor cried, and they tried to lighten the ship by throwing away their cargo, but that didn't work for them at all. During that situation, Jonah was below deck where he lay down and fell into a deep sleep.

6 The captain went to him and said, "How can you sleep? Get up and call on your God! Maybe He will take notice of us, and we will not perish."

The sailors decided to cast lots to find out who was responsible for the calamity. They did so, and the lot fell on Jonah. Jonah confessed everything, and he suggested they throw him into the sea. At first the sailors hesitated to throw him, but later they did it without option because the situation had grown worse. After that, everything became normal. Jonah was swallowed by a big fish, and it conveyed him to Nineveh, where he had decided not to go.

Check it out right now! Isn't this situation similar to the one in your family? Isn't your family in a trouble that God caused because of you? Your family is losing everything, trying to solve family problems. That's exactly what happened on the ship; the sailors lost their cargo because they wanted to lighten the ship so that it could not sink. Sometimes families suffer consequences because of a few individuals who are going against God's will. They unnecessarily pump out a lot of money and assets, trying to solve certain problems.

If you are Jonah on your family ship, do the will of God to save it. It's been a long time now; the members in your family are losing jobs, marriages, and so on. Do you want your family to die in that situation? Repent, and ask God to tell you what He really needs you to do.

Some people run away from serving God, and they decide to focus on their own careers without Him. They work hard in those careers, but they reap nothing. They receive a lot of money, but it doesn't solve their problems—it just vanishes. May God have mercy on us. Amen. Consider God in everything you do. When God says, "Do my work," He doesn't always mean you must be a pastor. *No.* You can preach for Him, whilst you are a soldier, a police officer, a nurse, a teacher, a contractor, a farmer, a vendor, an engineer, a doctor, a business person, or whatsoever.

Apart from creating situations to bring us to His will, God creates them to train us to be responsible enough for what He is going to give us. Papa Guti, the founder of the ZAOGA Forward in Faith Ministry, wrote a book titled *Human Beings Cannot Change without Pressure*. This is true. People cannot change without pressure. Situations change people's behaviour and responsibility. It is very important to have our behaviour worked before we receive God's gifts. When immature people receive gifts from God, pride attacks them, and many of them die before time. May God have mercy on us. Many men die because they fail to handle their riches. And in the same manner, many ladies die because they fail to handle their beauty. This is the reason God trains us before we receive His riches. Usually, when we are not ready, He doesn't give us.

Unlike God, the devil creates situations to hinder our dreams. Praise God! He converts the devil's hindrance into our success. Let's look at what happened to our fellows who were recorded in the Bible. Their challenges and success will definitely motivate us.

Challenges are always available with us on earth. It is so normal that we face them. Always remember that the devil does not bring these challenges to you in person; instead, he influences people with you. God also does the same.

From Professor Ezekiel Guti's *Human Beings Cannot Change without Pressure*, I learnt that there are outdoor and indoor challenges. The outdoor challenges are those challenges brought to us by the people whom we don't associate with, whereas the indoor ones are from those we always associate with.

These challenges make us mature in spirit, and they shape our behaviour. They bring us pressure, which pushes us to move for better. If we respond to this pressure negatively, it kills us either physically or spiritually.

You cannot just become a great person without a story. Joseph in the Bible is one of the stars to look at. He did not just become a man of God from nowhere. He went through some difficulties. He was once cast into a deep pit by his own brothers [Genesis 37 vs. 24]. Later on, he was sold from the pit to be a slave [Genesis 37 vs. 28]. In Egypt, he was accused of attempted rape [Genesis 39 vs. 14-18] and was put in prison for that.

Joseph suffered indoor challenges from his own brothers and from Potiphar's wife.

In churches, there are such challenges from our fellow church members. These ones are tougher and more painful than those we face from the people we don't associate with.

Sometimes you can see a church that sought you through preaching going against you. This is normal. It also happened to Elisha. Elisha was sought by Elijah [1 Kings 19 vs. 19-21], but after that came a certain occasion when the same man, Elijah, who had called him, began to send him away [2 Kings 2 vs. 1-6]. If Elisha was as impatient as many of us are today, he would not persist in following Elijah, and he would not get a double portion of Elijah's spirit [2 Kings 2 vs. 9-13]. Amen.

Dear friends, when you fall into various trials, count it all joy [James 1 vs. 2]. The Lord does not leave you alone when you are in trouble. Shadrach, Abednego and Meshach were not left alone in a pit of fire [Daniel 3 vs. 24-25]. This is what God does when the devil tries to kill you. Hallelujah.

In David's case, Saul, the very person who had called David to serve in his house [1 Samuel 17 vs. 21-22], tried to kill him [1 Samuel 19 vs. 9-10]. So don't worry about those people in your church who once showed you their love, which they don't have these days. People are people, and God is God.

You must always know that the more the presence of God intensifies, the more the troubles from the devil come. The devil is like a dog barking during the night; when it barks, it barks at moving things, not at stationary ones.

The devil mainly troubles those with whom God has great plans. When you are already cool in the Kingdom of God, he (the devil) has no big deal with you. Remember King Pharaoh and his men. They tried to kill all the Hebrew boys, but they saved the girls. Likewise, the devil and his followers seek to murder those who are hot in the 'things' of God, not those that are cool.

If you are a believer who goes smoothly all the way without any temptation, trial or test, you need to check your position. You might have already stopped burning in spirit. It is usual to face challenges as a believer, and it is unusual not to face them. Jesus Christ faced them. So why can't you?

Dear friends, challenges are not permitted by God to weaken us; they come to strengthen us. Hallelujah. So let us all persevere in order that we achieve our goals.

Samson was born a strong man, but he needed some provocation from his enemies (the Philistines) in order for him to use his power. One day, he caught 300 foxes, tied their tails to make a total number of 150 pairs, and then attached torches to their tails. The foxes ran across the fields of the Philistines and burnt them to ashes [Judges 15 vs. 4-5]. Samson did so because he had faced a challenge from his Philistine father in-law who had, on a wedding day, given his (Samson's) wife to his (Samson's) best man [Judges 14 vs. 20].

Your pace in life is determined by the situation you face. Challenges are like rungs on a ladder; they lead us up. If they are not available, we won't go up. May the Lord God strengthen us when we face them. Hallelujah.

Do you see it now? Every challenge or situation comes for a purpose. We are what we are today because of our past situations, and our present situations mostly predetermine our future.

God is great and awesome in every situation. When the devil throws spikes into our way, God converts them into steps or rungs to take us up. But when God Himself throws them into our way, He does so to train us how to fly.

SITUATIONS CAUSED BY HUMAN ERROR

Many people are in different (physical or spiritual) situations into which they were put by their friends, relatives, workmates, and so on. They now live in regret. Many of them are so bitter that they even doubt the existence of God, and sometimes they think of committing suicide. This is the right time for God to show them His hand.

Some people are physically crippled today because of human error; they got involved in serious accidents, and now they are unable to work for themselves and for their families. They are usually despised and rejected by many people in their communities, but there is God in Heaven, who considers them day and night. Glory be unto Him.

Someone in the Bible to talk about is Mephibosheth, the son of Jonathan. He physically got crippled in both feet because of human error. During war, a maid accidentally dropped him when she was running away for their dear lives. People despised him, but God remembered him.

2 Samuel, chapter 9 [David and Mephibosheth]

1 David asked, "Is there anyone still left of the house of Saul to whom I can show kindness for Jonathan's sake?"

2 Now there was a servant of Saul's household named Ziba. They called him to appear before David, and the king said to him, "Are you Ziba?"

"Your servant," he replied.

3 The king asked, "Is there no-one still left of the house of Saul to whom I can show God's kindness?"

Ziba answered the king, "There is still a son of Jonathan; he is crippled in both feet."

Do you notice Ziba's reply? He added that Mephibosheth was crippled. There are always some people who say negative things against you whenever something good is to be done for you. The other thing is Ziba told the king that the only person left was Mephibosheth, yet there were other people of the household of Saul still surviving; you will see this at the end. Ziba mentioned Mephibosheth because he anticipated that the king would reject him because of his condition, and he dreamed of the king's favour coming on his (Ziba's) side.

Contrary to Ziba's expectation, 4 the king asked, "Where is he?"

Ziba answered, "He is at the house of Makir son of Ammiel in Lo Debar."

5 So King David had him brought from Lo Debar, from the house of Makir son of Ammiel.

6 When Mephibosheth son of Jonathan, the son of Saul, came to David, he bowed down to pay him honour.

David said, "Mephibosheth!"

"Your servant," he replied.

7 "Don't be afraid," David said to him, "for I will surely show you kindness for the sake of your father Jonathan. I will restore to you all the land that belonged to your grandfather Saul, and you will always eat at my table."

This time around, God is going to show you favour. Don't worry about this deadly situation into which your friend, relative or workmate put you. God is going to rub off all your tears, and He is going to restore all that was taken away from you. Glory be unto Him.

In the case of Mephibosheth, God's favour did not only end there, but it extended to save him from other situations.

2 Samuel, chapter 21 [The Gibeonites Avenged]

1 During the reign of David, there was a famine for three successive years; so David sought the face of the Lord. The Lord said, "It is on account of Saul and his blood-stained house; it is because he put the Gibeonites to death."

This is another pandemic situation in life caused by human error. Many people are suffering because someone else in their family murdered innocent blood some time ago. This is what we call *kuripira ngozi* (to appease avenging spirits).

2 The king summoned the Gibeonites and spoke to them. (Now the Gibeonites were not a part of Israel but were survivors of the Amorites; the Israelites had sworn to spare them, but Saul in his zeal for Israel and Judah had tried to annihilate them.) **3** David asked the

Gibeonites, "What shall I do for you? How shall I make amends so that you will bless the Lord's inheritance?"

4 The Gibeonites answered him, "We have no right to demand silver or gold from Saul or his family, nor do we have the right to put anyone in Israel to death."

"What do you want me to do for you?" David asked.

5 They answered the king, "As for the man who destroyed us and plotted against us so that we have been decimated and have no place anywhere in Israel, 6 let seven of his male descendants be given to us to be killed and exposed before the Lord at Gibeah of Saul—the Lord's chosen one."

So the king said, "I will give them to you."

7 The king spared Mephibosheth son of Jonathan, the son of Saul, because of the oath before the Lord between David and Jonathan son of Saul. 8 But the king took Armoni and Mephibosheth, the two sons of Aiah's daughter Rizpah, whom she had borne to Saul, together with the five sons of Saul's daughter Merab, whom she had borne to Adriel son of Barzillai the Meholathite. 9 He handed them over to the Gibeonites, who killed and exposed them on a hill before the Lord. All seven of them fell together; they were put to death during the first days of harvest, just as the barley harvest was beginning.

Do you now see it?—It was not true when Ziba said the only person left in the household of Saul was Mephibosheth, the son of Jonathan. There were still others including another Mephibosheth, the son of Saul.

Dear friends, *ngozi* (a spiritual trouble caused by avenging spirits) exists, but it does not affect those that received Jesus Christ as their personal saviour. This is so because God made an oath with Jesus Christ that He would spare anyone who would receive Him (Jesus Christ). See, there were two people with the same name 'Mephibosheth' in the same household, but one of them was saved, while the other one perished. Mephibosheth the son of Jonathan was spared from appeasing the avenging spirits because of the oath between David and his (Mephibosheth's) father. Though you are of the same blood with your family members, you are spared from appeasing these avenging spirits *(kuripira ngozi)* because of the oath between God and your Jesus Christ. From today onwards, you must always know that you are not a candidate of *ngozi* in your family. Hallelujah. Don't be equally yoked with unbelievers: 2 Corinthians 6 vs. 14: Do not be yoked together with unbelievers. For what do righteousness and wickedness have in common? Or what fellowship can light have with darkness?

Say no to *ngozi*. Tell the devil that he is lost to count you one of the *ngozi* victims in your family. Because of Christ, you are no longer bound in any situation caused by human error. Amen.

The devil takes advantage of you because you don't read the Word of God, and you have got little knowledge about your freedom.

If there is anyone who has never received Jesus Christ as their personal saviour, take this time to receive Him. Your blood needs to be spiritually diluted with the blood of Jesus Christ. Without the blood of Jesus, your blood alone is the mode of transport for principalities.

Principalities [Eph. 6 vs. 12] are demonic spirits that have been operating from ancient times. They trace family blood, introducing and passing on negative principles of life from one or more members of an extended family to the other. This is why you see some people face certain situations which were once faced by their ancestors.

The principalities that affect family A are different from those that affect family B. This is why you see family A has got educated members, but no one of them is allowed to get a good job. If anyone gets employed, they die or become mad. But family B is different; its members are not educated, but they do well in life. If anyone in family B gets educated, they die or become mad.

Family C has got its different situation; every member is educated and employed, but they don't get married.

You see? You have to receive Jesus Christ to get rid of these spirits. That's why I said your blood needs to be spiritually diluted with the blood of Jesus Christ. Amen.

JESUS CHRIST IN YOUR SITUATION

Matthew 11 vs. 28-30: **28** "Come to me, all you who are weary and burdened, and I will give you rest. **29** Take my yoke upon you and learn from me, for I am gentle and humble in heart, and you will find rest for your souls. **30** For my yoke is easy and my burden is light."

These are Jesus Christ's words. Jesus is the answer to everything. He is the one to break up every chain that tied you and to offload any burden from you. If He sets you free, you will be free indeed [John 8 vs. 36].

He is the only way and the truth to God the Father [John, chapter 10]. Glory be unto Him. Amen.

This Jesus Christ is the one to call for any situation. One day, He was on a boat with His disciples, and they were sailing across a very big lake. As they sailed, a violent storm started up on the lake, and it forced waves to shake the boat. By that time, Jesus was sleeping; meanwhile, His disciples were struggling in the storm situation. The waves caused much water to splash into the boat, and it (the boat) was about to sink. The disciples tried to scoop it out, but it never stopped coming in. Finally, the disciples remembered to call Jesus for their growing situation. Jesus woke up and rebuked the storm, and it died down forthwith [Mark 4 vs. 35-41].

Dear friends, Jesus Christ is always around. When you are in trouble, call Him. If you don't call unto Him, you die in it, whilst He is present. If the disciples did not acknowledge Him, they would continue in trouble.

A certain woman was in a bleeding situation for 12 years. She tried every medical practitioner, but they failed her. She wasted a lot of money and property, trying to solve the problem. One day, faith drove her to touch just a hem of Jesus' garment. When she touched it, the bleeding stopped right there [Mark 5 vs. 25-29]. Sometimes you don't need someone to tell you what to do with your situation. Your own decision and faith can save you. It's not always that a pastor should lay hands on you. Right?

Jesus Christ is always awesome in every situation. There is also a time when He fed about 5,000 people with five loaves of bread and two fish [Mark 6 vs. 30-44]. He is able to transform the little you have into something big, and He is going to do it. The little business you have is going to be changed into an enormous business, and this will astonish many people. Hallelujah!

Miracles continued after Jesus ascended to Heaven. He left us with the Holy Spirit, and, through it, we continue to perform these things. One day, Peter and John, the disciples that Jesus Christ physically left on earth, healed a man born crippled.

Acts, chapter 3 [Peter Heals the Crippled Beggar]

1 One day Peter and John were going up to the temple at the time of prayer—at three in the afternoon. **2** Now a man crippled from birth was being carried to the temple gate called Beautiful, where he was put every day to beg from those going into the temple courts. **3** When he saw Peter and John about to enter, he asked them for money. **4** Peter looked straight at him, as did John. Then Peter said, "Look at us!" **5** So the man gave them his attention, expecting to get something from them.

6 Then Peter said, "Silver or gold I do not have, but what I have I give you. In the name of Jesus Christ of Nazareth, walk." **7** Taking him by the right hand, he helped him up, and instantly the man's feet and ankles became strong. **8** He jumped to his feet and began to walk. Then he went with them into the temple courts, walking and jumping, and praising God. **9** When all the people saw him walking and praising God, **10** they recognised him as the same man who used to sit begging at the temple gate called Beautiful, and they were filled with wonder and amazement at what had happened to him.

Indeed, that was awesome. Do you understand this story? The man was in the situation from his mother's womb. This is pathetic. He was of the same age with his problem, and he was used to living in it. His relatives took advantage of him, and they used him for begging.

We have got such people right now. They were born initiated from their mothers' wombs. They were given spiritual husbands and wives. Some of them were initiated to be witches and wizards. May God have mercy on them. Some are mentally challenged, and their relatives take advantage of them. This is over! Run to Jesus Christ for your salvation.

Jesus Christ is the answer to your situations. Amen. The definition of your situation is in Him. God is still using His servants to deliver people, and His miracles still exist.

God bless you in Jesus Christ's name, amen!

CLOSING PRAYER

God, the Almighty Warrior, who dwells between the cherubim, great and awesome is your name Jehovah, the Almighty.

I thank you for your Word about my situation.

May your peace and teachings dwell in me, forever and ever, in Jesus Christ's name. Amen.

CITATION

1. Guti, E.H. (2006). *Human Beings Cannot Change without Pressure*. Harare, Zimbabwe: EGEA.

—The End—